Here We Go...

Thank you again for taking the first steps toward unlocking your potential. If you have this guide, I'm assuming you've already purchased the book and you are ready to move from STUCK to UNSTOPPABLE. Although the exercises in this workbook are also outlined in the **Unlock Your Potential** book, I'm thinking ahead for those women who prefer to keep the beautiful pages of your books clear and free of any writing and marks.

This workbook is a more convenient way to complete the exercises as you finish reading about each action in **Unlock Your Potential**. Once you complete all the exercises, you can quickly turn back through these workbook pages and reflect on your progress. I may not know you yet, but I'm always thinking of you, and I've got your back.
YOU CAN DO THIS!

- Kimberly

ACTION #1
Examine Your Past

1. List a few times in your life when things didn't turn out like you wanted them to.
   _____
   _____
   _____
   _____
   _____
   _____
   _____
   _____

2. Review the incidents you jotted down. For each one, is there something you could've done differently to have avoided or mitigated the results? Think of at least one lesson you learned from those painful experiences and write them down so you don't double-dip.
   _____
   _____
   _____
   _____

3. Based on what you could've done differently in the past, list three changes you can make in your life to apply the lesson you learned.
   _____
   _____
   _____

4. Look at those changes you listed in Question #3 and write down only the changes that are long-term benefits for you.
   _____
   _____
   _____

BONUS.

Use your imagination. Take one of those past situations you listed in #1 and rewrite it with yourself taking the action you noted in #2. What possible outcomes do you see? This is what's possible when you stop repeating past mistakes.

_____
_____
_____
_____
_____
_____
_____
_____
_____
_____

You're welcome to add anything else in this section that might help you to examine your past.

_____
_____
_____
_____
_____
_____
_____

ACTION #2
Use What You Already Have

The easiest way to identify your best skill sets is to ask yourself a few questions. And if you are 100% HONEST with yourself, you will find the answers you need. Don't worry if you have the same answer for a few of the questions, most people do. And don't allow yourself more than a few seconds to answer.

1. What do you enjoy doing outside of work?

   _____
   _____
   _____
   _____
   _____

2. What could you talk about into the night, with like-minded people, without running out of things to say?

   _____
   _____
   _____
   _____
   _____

3. What specific talents are you known for at work (co-workers know to turn to you if they have a question about this topic)?

   _____
   _____
   _____
   _____
   _____

4. What abilities are you known for among your family and friends?

_____
_____
_____
_____
_____

5. What skill(s) have you mastered so well, you could teach others how to do it?

_____
_____
_____
_____
_____

6. What task makes you feel useful, alive, strong (when are you in your zone)?

_____
_____
_____
_____
_____

7. If money wasn't a factor, what would you be doing with your skills
   5 years from now?

_____
_____
_____
_____
_____

ACTION #2 (cont.)
Use What You Already Have

8. From your answers on page 26, circle at least two skills you already have that you could be using to help you reach new goals. Write them down here:

   _____
   _____
   _____
   _____
   _____
   _____
   _____

9. Briefly describe what goals those skills and talents could be helping you work towards.

   _____
   _____
   _____
   _____
   _____
   _____
   _____
   _____
   _____

10. Write one small action step you can take now, using your unique talents, to start working towards one of your goals.

    _____
    _____
    _____
    _____
    _____
    _____
    _____

11. For the action step you identified in #10, schedule it on your calendar. On what day will you start using what you have?
   _____

12. Take a few minutes to brainstorm what your dream is. Think about how it will benefit you and those you care about to use your skills and uplift that dream.
   _____
   _____
   _____
   _____
   _____
   _____
   _____
   _____
   _____

You're welcome to add anything else in this section that might help you to start using what you already have.
_____
_____
_____
_____
_____
_____
_____
_____

ACTION #3
Think BIG

1. Brainstorm the things in your life right now that you consider "good enough."

   _____
   _____
   _____
   _____
   _____

2. Of the things you listed, which ones make you feel less than you know you're capable of?

   _____
   _____
   _____
   _____

3. What are the barriers you face because of settling for this "good enough" version of yourself?

   _____
   _____
   _____
   _____

4. What changes can you make to surround yourself with more successful people and think bigger? Write everything that comes to mind.

   _____
   _____
   _____
   _____

5. Of the possible changes you came up with, choose three changes that you can commit to do now and write them below:

   "I commit to do _____, _____ and _____ in the next 30 days.

6. Imagine what your life will be like when you're swimming with bigger fish. Write about a dinner party with the amazingly successful people you'll be surrounded with. What opportunities will arise from that occasion?
The sky is the limit.

_____
_____
_____
_____
_____
_____
_____

You're welcome to add anything else in this section that might help you to think big.

_____
_____
_____
_____
_____
_____
_____

ACTION #4
Reframe Your Guilt

1. Think about a few times that you've felt guilty. Who was there, what was at stake, and how did the situation turn out? Choose 2-3 that stand out to you and list them below.

   _____
   _____
   _____
   _____
   _____
   _____
   _____

2. For what you listed above, do you notice any commonalities between those times you felt guilty? Look for patterns when the same things happened in different situations. It might be the same people or circumstances or issues, etc. Write those patterns down.

   _____
   _____
   _____
   _____
   _____
   _____
   _____

3. For the patterns of guilt you identified, list some actions you could take to avoid those patterns going forward.

   _____
   _____
   _____
   _____
   _____
   _____
   _____

4. Of the actions you listed in #3, which one are you going to commit to take now to change those patterns of guilt and put yourself first?

_____
_____
_____
_____
_____
_____
_____

5. Reflect on how getting rid of guilt will help you in the future and write briefly about the ways you think your life could be different without guilt.

_____
_____
_____
_____
_____
_____
_____

You're welcome to add anything else in this section that might help you reframe your guilt.

_____
_____
_____
_____
_____
_____
_____

ACTION #5
Respond with Boundaries and Compassion

1. Brainstorm all the things in your life that you currently say "yes," to.

   _____
   _____
   _____
   _____
   _____
   _____
   _____

2. Review each of the things you're saying "yes," to above. List the ones that don't make you feel good because you're too tired for them, they stress you out, they require too much of your time, they don't align with your values, etc.

   _____
   _____
   _____
   _____
   _____
   _____
   _____

3. Choose at least two things that you listed above and commit to saying "no" to them. Write the sentence below:

   "I commit that next time I'm asked to _____, I will say 'no.'"

   "I commit that next time I'm asked to _____, I will say 'no.'"

4. For all the things you that you're saying "yes," to that don't make you feel good (question 2), notice what you might be able to do differently to avoid agreeing to do those things. Consider boundaries you might set, and list 2-3 actions you can take.

_____
_____
_____
_____
_____
_____

5. The best thing about not saying "yes," to everything is that you create more room in your life to say "yes," to what you want. What are the things you'll be able to say "yes" to now? List a few of the good things you're looking forward to.

_____
_____
_____
_____
_____
_____
_____

You're welcome to add anything else in this section that might help you to respond with boundaries and compassion.

_____
_____
_____
_____
_____

ACTION #6
Protect Your Heart

1. What are 2-3 compliments that you get the most often from your biggest supporters who love and understand you? Depending on where you are now, this might be family members, peers, or customers.

   _____
   _____
   _____
   _____
   _____
   _____
   _____

2. What are 2-3 things these people also have in common with each other?

   _____
   _____
   _____
   _____
   _____
   _____
   _____

3. Where do these people hang out most often? Online or in-person.

   _____
   _____
   _____
   _____
   _____
   _____
   _____

4. What can you do to put yourself in situations to meet more people like the ones who appreciate you?

_____
_____
_____
_____
_____
_____
_____

5. Brainstorm the new opportunities that might come your way when you become a magnet for those people who like you.

_____
_____
_____
_____
_____
_____
_____

You're welcome to add anything else in this section that might help you to protect your heart.

_____
_____
_____
_____
_____
_____
_____

ACTION #7
Recruit A Trusted Advisor

1. Think back through your life at the times you were most successful. In each of those times, who was cheering you on?

   _____
   _____
   _____
   _____
   _____
   _____

2. Look at your life now. Who are the people around you that are still playing those same supportive roles for you now?

   _____
   _____
   _____
   _____
   _____
   _____

3. Are there some gaps in your support system? Who are some people that played roles in your previous success that aren't there for you now?

   _____
   _____
   _____
   _____
   _____
   _____

4. Who are some people that have not played a role in your previous success, but you want to have them there in the future?

   _____
   _____
   _____
   _____

5. Brainstorm some things you can do to surround yourself with more successfuland encouraging people. Who can you trust with your megaphone?

_____
_____
_____
_____
_____
_____

6. Of the things you considered in #5, choose the one that seems the most doable and likely to succeed. Then, write the follow sentence:

"I commit to do _____ to have more successful people in my life to encourage me."

7. When your life is filled with supportive people, there will be no room for the people that aren't supportive. Think about what it will be like to go after your goals without the negative people in your cheering section. What's going to be possible for you?

_____
_____
_____
_____

You're welcome to add anything else in this section that might help you to fill your cheering section with positive energy and support.

_____
_____
_____
_____
_____

ACTION #8
Delegate

1. Think about the last month. When did you wish you had help with something? What are those tasks you struggled to do on your own, due to time, capabilities, priorities, etc?

   _____
   _____
   _____
   _____
   _____
   _____

2. Not doing everything by yourself is about knowing who to ask for help and how to ask for it. For each of the tasks you listed above, brainstorm all the possible people you could ask to help you with each one.

   _____
   _____
   _____
   _____
   _____
   _____

3. Of the people you listed, consider which person is most capable for each task and how they can possibly benefit from completing the task. List them below.

   _____
   _____
   _____
   _____
   _____
   _____

4. Find the words you'll use to ask these people for help next time you need it. Practice saying those words in a mirror, so you'll be confident.

_____
_____
_____
_____
_____
_____

5. How is it going to benefit you when you're delegating tasks and not doing everything by yourself? What are you going to have more time for? Be intentional, because otherwise you can make time for more busy work instead of more activities that will help you unlock your potential.

_____
_____
_____
_____
_____
_____

You're welcome to add anything else in this section that might help you to delegate.

_____
_____
_____
_____
_____
_____

ACTION #9
Identify Your Lifters and Thrusters

1. Think about the people you spend the majority of your time with—Family, Friends, Your Spouse, Co-workers, Neighbors, etc. Write them all down (first names or initials).

   _____
   _____
   _____
   _____
   _____

2. Identify the people who meet the definition of drags and weights and write them down. Explain what they have done to be put in this category.

   _____
   _____
   _____
   _____
   _____

3. Of the people you listed above, write down how their negativity has affected you.

   _____
   _____
   _____
   _____
   _____

4. Identify at least three people who have lifted you up and thrusted you forward.

   _____
   _____
   _____
   _____

5. What goals are you working toward now that you'd like support from your lifters and thrusters? Write this down:

I am working on _____ and I will call on _____ to support me with _____."

I am working on _____ and I will call on _____ to support me with _____."

6. Take your list of lifters and thrusters and add their phone numbers and email addresses below so you have them in reach:

_____
_____
_____
_____
_____
_____
_____
_____

You're welcome to add anything else in this section that might help you to surround yourself with lifters and thrusters, and spend less time with drags and weights.

_____
_____
_____
_____
_____
_____
_____

ACTION #10
Put Yourself Out There

1. What would "putting yourself out there" look like for you? Is it being more visible on social media, networking, speaking, blogging, writing articles, making videos, having a podcast, attending live events, etc.?

   _____
   _____
   _____
   _____
   _____

2. For the ways to put yourself out there that you listed above, briefly write why you're not already doing those things.

   _____
   _____
   _____
   _____
   _____

3. Look at what you just wrote. How many of those reasons are about fear? What are those fears?

   _____
   _____
   _____
   _____
   _____

   For the fears you listed, are any of them truly life-threatening? If they're like mine, those fears are about what others will say or think about me. Cross out those fears. Look how many disappeared!

   _____
   _____
   _____
   _____

4. Look at your answers in #1. Which of those ways are you willing to commit to? Write it down.

_____
_____
_____
_____

5. What actions would you need to take to make your answers in #4 happen?

_____
_____
_____
_____

6. Choose one action from #5 and commit to it.
"I commit to do _____

in order to put myself out there."

_____
_____
_____
_____

7. When you put yourself out there, you need your words to be effective. How are you going to speak about yourself?

_____
_____
_____
_____

You're welcome to add anything else in this section that might help you to put yourself out there.

_____
_____

ACTION #11
Listen Before You Speak

1. Review the relationships that are important to you. In which of those relationships do you do most of the talking?

2. Who are the people in your life that you could be listening to more?

3. What are two relationships you can improve by listening more and speaking less?

4. How would you describe your current listening skills?

5. In what ways can you work to improve your current listening skills?

6. How would you describe your body language when you're speaking?
_____
_____
_____
_____

7. What are you going to watch for in your nonverbal communication to make sure you are speaking in the way you want to be received?
_____
_____
_____
_____
_____

8. How will all of the above changes lead you to unlock more of your potential?
_____
_____
_____
_____
_____
_____
_____

You're welcome to add anything else in this section that might help you to improve your listening skills and your nonverbal communication.
_____
_____
_____
_____
_____

ACTION #12
Be Patient

1. Brainstorm all the problems you currently face—big and small.

   _____
   _____
   _____
   _____
   _____
   _____
   _____
   _____

2. Consider which of these problems you wish were solved right now and circle them.

   _____
   _____
   _____
   _____
   _____
   _____
   _____
   _____

3. For the problems you circled, what do you think is making you feel impatient to solve those problems? Briefly describe:

   _____
   _____
   _____
   _____
   _____
   _____
   _____

4. Now that you have a good picture of your impatience, what can you do for those problems, to move yourself in the ultimate direction of your goals? VERY SMALL actions.

_____
_____
_____
_____

5. Once those small actions above are complete, what can you do next? You're still thinking small—two more actions.

_____
_____
_____
_____

    Once those two actions are done, what's next?

_____
_____
_____
_____

6. How will your patience lead you to make progress on those problems? Maybe even some other ones, too?

_____
_____
_____

You're welcome to add anything else in this section that might help you to be more patient.

_____
_____
_____
_____

ACTION #13
Focus

Distractions

1. Think about the current tasks on your plate, and write down the ones you're most focused on.

   _____
   _____
   _____
   _____

2. For each of those tasks, what are the distractions that are preventing you from moving forward as you would like (people, things, excuses, habits, etc)?

   _____
   _____
   _____
   _____

3. What impact are these distractions making on your ability to unlock your potential?

   _____
   _____
   _____
   _____

4. What steps can you take to limit these distractions in the future?

   _____
   _____
   _____
   _____

Electronic Communications

1. In what way is electronic communication controlling how you spend your time (emails, IM, text, etc.)?

   _____
   _____
   _____
   _____

2. Which platforms do you feel you have a handle on, and which ones constantly interrupt your day and suck away your time and attention?

   _____
   _____
   _____
   _____

3. Why do these distractions have so much power over your day-to-day?

   _____
   _____
   _____
   _____

4. What three changes can you make to stop letting electronic communication control you?

   _____
   _____
   _____
   _____

5. How will you benefit from not letting emails and social media distract you? Briefly write about what it's going to be like for you to do everything you'll be able to do in one ideal day without distractions.

   _____
   _____
   _____

ACTION #14
Control Your Social

1. Has there been a time that you saw something on social media that made you feel bad or like you were missing out? Describe what you saw and how you felt.

   _____
   _____
   _____
   _____
   _____
   _____
   _____

   Did it make you do anything you otherwise wouldn't have?

   _____
   _____
   _____
   _____

   How did that turn out for you?

   _____
   _____
   _____
   _____

2. Plan your social media time. What platforms will you be on?

   _____
   _____
   _____
   _____

   What time will you check into the platforms?

   _____
   _____
   _____

Whose social media accounts lift you up, that you want to keep following?

_____
_____
_____
_____

Who will you unfriend or unfollow so they don't keep affecting you?

_____
_____
_____
_____

How will you stick to your new boundaries with social media when you see things that would've caused FOMO?

_____
_____
_____
_____

3. What will be different in your life when you control your social media engagement strategy?

_____
_____
_____
_____

You're welcome to add anything else in this section that might help you to control your social.

_____
_____
_____
_____

ACTION #15
Develop Healthy Habits

1. What's your daily routine now? Briefly outline your typical day. Think about what you do, where you go, what and how much you eat, etc.

   6:00 a.m. _____

   9:00 a.m. _____

   12:00 p.m. _____

   3:00 p.m. _____

   6:00 p.m. _____

   9:00 p.m. _____

2. What are the healthy things you're doing that you want to continue?

   _____
   _____
   _____
   _____

3. What are the unhealthy things you're doing that you know could be better?

   _____
   _____
   _____
   _____

4. Name at least two healthy changes that you would like to add to your daily routine. For both, when do you see that you can add them into your day?

   _____
   _____
   _____
   _____

5. How healthy are you—really? Describe the state of your health. Think about any areas of your body where you might have chronic pain, ongoing medication, limited abilities, and other health concerns.

_____
_____
_____
_____

6. It's very common for over-achieving people to let your health suffer because of your work habits. What work habits could you change, which might positively impact some of your health concerns?

_____
_____
_____
_____

7. Close your eyes and imagine how your body will feel better when you're introducing more healthy habits. What new things will you be able to do?

_____
_____
_____
_____

8. When you feel better and have more energy, how is that going to help you unlock your potential?

_____
_____
_____
_____

ACTION #16
Ask For Help

1. Name one or two areas of your life where you could use a mentor or a coach.
   _____
   _____

2. Consider these three criteria of needs to determine if you need a mentor or a coach. Circle the kinds of help you need most now with your goal:
   - a. long-term help
   - b. short-term help
   - a. general assistance
   - b. specific assistance
   - a. professional development
   - b. strengthen a specific skillset

   If you selected mostly a's, you need a mentor
   If you selected mostly b's, you need a coach

3. It's time to find your coach or mentor. Who do you know that could give you that support, or who can you ask to give you a referral?
   _____
   _____
   _____
   _____
   _____

4. What actions will you take to establish this new relationship?
   _____
   _____
   _____
   _____
   _____

5. What are your goals for working with your coach or mentor?

_____
_____
_____
_____
_____

6. How will reaching these goals help you unlock your potential?

_____
_____
_____
_____
_____

You're welcome to add anything else in this section that might encourage you to ask for help.

_____
_____
_____
_____
_____
_____
_____

ACTION #17
Let Go of Perfectionism

1. Take a minute for self-reflection. Would you call yourself a perfectionist? What makes you think so?

   _____
   _____
   _____

   Have others ever called you a perfectionist, over-achiever, OCD, or Type-A? If so, what made them say that?

   _____
   _____
   _____

   Think of a moment when you were driven by perfectionism. How did you feel, and what thoughts went through your head?

   _____
   _____
   _____

   Circle anything you wrote above that counts as a fear.

   How did the task turn out in the end? Were those fears valid?

   _____
   _____
   _____

2. List at least 2-3 goals you would set for yourself if you weren't afraid you wouldn't accomplish those things perfectly.

   _____
   _____
   _____

For each goal listed, what's the best thing that could happen if it goes well?

_____
_____
_____

What actions will you commit to do to overcome your fear and get started? Write your statement:

"I commit to _____, _____, and _____ to make progress despite my fears."

3. Close your eyes and imagine that you've successfully completed a goal from #2. What will it feel like after you let go of the fears that make you a perfectionist?

_____
_____
_____
_____
_____

What would that new version of yourself say to you where you are now?

_____
_____
_____
_____

You're welcome to add anything else in this section that might help you to let go of fear and perfectionism.

_____
_____
_____
_____

ACTION #18
Start Small

1. Think big and without limitations. List 5 things you'd like to accomplish:
   _____
   _____
   _____
   _____
   _____

2. Taking a good look at your list above, let's narrow down what to start working on first. Look at your list of what you want to accomplish, and as best as you can, put your it in order of what would need to happen first, second and third. List them below. A lot of times, success is a domino effect. For example, if you want to be on Oprah's Soul Sunday, you might want to finish writing your book first.

3. What are the first 3 goals you want to achieve?
   1. _____
   2. _____
   3. _____

4. For the first goal, how long will it take to complete it?
   What are all the actions you'll need to take to achieve that goal?

   Goal #1 is _____
   it will take me _____ days/months/years. Steps I need to take to accomplish this goal: _____ _____ _____

   Goal #2 is _____
   it will take me _____ days/months/years. Steps I need to take to accomplish this goal: _____ _____ _____

   Goal #3 is _____
   it will take me _____ days/months/years. Steps I need to take to accomplish this goal: _____ _____ _____

5. With your three goals in mind, we're going to find time to get them done. List everything going on in your life that might come first in front of the goals.

   _____
   _____
   _____

6. For each obstacle you listed, what can you do to overcome it? Use your new skills you've learned like delegating, saying no, and setting boundaries.

   _____
   _____
   _____

7. Look at your calendar and block time to work on your goal. Write it here, too. What days and times of day will you spend on your goal until you complete it?

   _____
   _____
   _____

8. What will change in your life when you accomplish your first goal? Second and third?

   _____
   _____
   _____

9. How will your progress and key changes in your life lead you to unlock your potential?

   _____
   _____
   _____
   _____

ACTION #19
Lead By Following

1. In what areas of your life are you a leader?

   What's going well for you in those areas where you lead?

   What would you like to be better?

   How could shifting your position to being a follower in these areas improve the situation?

2. Consider the things you listed that you would like to be better. Who are the other people present in those areas?

_____
_____
_____
_____

Which of these people are following instead of leading?

_____
_____
_____
_____

What can you do to give the people you listed as followers an opportunity to lead?

_____
_____
_____
_____

3. What are the possibilities you see for yourself and others when you're being a follower more often?

_____
_____
_____
_____

You're welcome to add anything else in this section that might help you to lead by following.

_____
_____
_____
_____

ACTION #20
Analyze Your Comparisons

1. List everything in your life you have ever overcome or achieved.

   _____
   _____
   _____
   _____
   _____
   _____
   _____
   _____
   _____

2. That's not all. Keep writing. Go through school, all the way to today, and list more achievements.

   _____
   _____
   _____
   _____
   _____

3. List 2-3 people you regularly compare yourself to.

   _____
   _____
   _____
   _____

4. Looking at the people you listed above (in #3), describe how you feel when you think about each of them and what they've accomplished that you wish you had done, too.

   _____
   _____
   _____
   _____
   _____

5. Look at everything you wrote for #1. What have you overcome or accomplished that the people you listed in #3 possibly haven't?

_____
_____
_____
_____
_____
_____

6. What will you change about how you see yourself so you can stop unhelpful comparisons?

_____
_____
_____
_____
_____
_____

7. How will your life improve when you quit competing with others?

_____
_____
_____
_____
_____
_____

You're welcome to add anything else in this section that might help you to analyze your comparisons.

_____
_____
_____
_____

ACTION #21
Take Responsibility

1. List the major excuses you've made about why you haven't been more successful over the years:

   _____
   _____
   _____
   _____

2. When you look at those excuses, how many of them did you previously think were reasons? For each, what changed so that you now see those statements as excuses?

   _____
   _____
   _____
   _____

3. Name one excuse that you still think is valid:

   _____

   What goals is that excuse preventing you from achieving?

   _____
   _____
   _____

4. What actions could you take to overcome the excuse? List at least three possible actions you can take.

   _____
   _____
   _____

5. Of the three actions you listed in #4, why haven't you done those things already? What's holding you back?

   _____
   _____
   _____

6. It's time to reframe the excuse you wrote in #3. Write a statement about the excuse in the opposite. For example, if the excuse is, "I don't have time to start a business because I'm a mom," rewrite it to say, "I do have time to start a business because I'm a mom."

_____
_____
_____
_____

7. **Take action:** Write your new statement on a Post-it Note. Put that note where you will see it every day and say that statement aloud to yourself until you memorize and believe it.

_____
_____

8. What are all the ways you will benefit when you no longer give in to your excuses?

_____
_____
_____
_____
_____

9. Without excuses, what potential are you going to unlock?

_____
_____
_____

You're welcome to add anything else in this section that might help you to stop making excuses and start where you are today.

_____
_____
_____
_____

Let's Continue Your Journey Together.

The Community

Action #9 discussed a need to surround yourself with people who will Lift you up and Thrust you toward your potential. I want you to succeed in this area, so I've already assembled your Dream Team for you. If you are ready to join a community of positive women who are unlocking their full potential, we have a resource for you.

Join the Private Community

Are you ready to **implement positive changes** and become the **BEST version of yourself?** Then the **Unlock Your Potential Community** is for you. Whatever you desire most, our private network can help you **move from stuck... to unstoppable!**

Connect with other women, **receive inspiration and support,** and gain access to dozens of exclusive **trainings and resources** to help keep you motivated and ensure you are using your unique skill sets to get to the next level. Plus, members receive exclusive previews of new products and **special discounts.**

Learn more at **kimberlybuchanan.com**

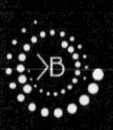

About Kimberly

Kimberly Buchanan is an international bestselling author, speaker, certified transformation coach and award-winning corporate professional. She is also a wife, mom and mentor to a community of amazing women.

Best known for helping ambitious and courageous women make an impact on the world, Kimberly provides valuable content, training and transformation coaching to help them overcome their fears and use their talents and skill set to reach new goals beyond their day jobs.

Kimberly gained her experience working as a trusted consultant for some of the largest, global companies in the world including Daimler Chrysler, Discover Card, Accenture, Pfizer and many others. She has appeared in newspapers, on television and nationally syndicated radio programs.

Kimberly has also contributed her productivity, business and work/life balance expertise to national publications, including *Forbes, Thrive Global* and *The Huffington Post,* and speaks frequently at seminars and conferences.

She currently resides in Illinois with her husband and their two sons. You can find her online at **kimberlybuchanan.com**, on **Instagram**, **Twitter and LinkedIn @kimsbuchanan**, and on **Facebook @kimsbuchanan1**.

HOW TO CONTACT KIMBERLY

Kimberly is committed to sharing the very best of what she is living and learning with you.

FOR INTERVIEWS, KEYNOTES AND WORKSHOPS:

Email: **info@kimberlybuchanan.com**
Online: **kimberlybuchanan.com**

SIGN UP for Kimberly's email list and join the Private Community at kimberlybuchanan.com

TO PURCHASE bulk copies of this book at a discount for your group or organization, please email **info@kimberlybuchanan.com**

www.ingramcontent.com/pod-product-compliance
Lightning Source LLC
Chambersburg PA
CBHW071416290426
44108CB00014B/1853